Scale Studies
(One String)
for the Violin

Part One

One-Octave
Scales

by Cassia Harvey

CHP178

©2007 by C. Harvey Publications All Rights Reserved.
6403 N. 6th Street
Philadelphia, PA 19126
www.charveypublications.com

F major

E string

by Cassia Harvey
edited by Myanna Harvey

Scale Studies (One String) for the Violin, Part One: One-Octave Scales

©2007 C. Harvey Publications All Rights Reserved.

Scale Studies (One String) for the Violin, Part One: One-Octave Scales

B♭ major

A string

Scale Studies (One String) for the Violin, Part One: One-Octave Scales

Scale Studies (One String) for the Violin, Part One: One-Octave Scales ©2007 C. Harvey Publications All Rights Reserved.

E♭ major

D string

Scale Studies (One String) for the Violin, Part One: One-Octave Scales ©2007 C. Harvey Publications All Rights Reserved.

A♭ major

G string

Scale Studies (One String) for the Violin, Part One: One-Octave Scales ©2007 C. Harvey Publications All Rights Reserved.

Scale Studies (One String) for the Violin, Part One: One-Octave Scales
©2007 C. Harvey Publications All Rights Reserved.

F major

E string

Scale Studies (One String) for the Violin, Part One: One-Octave Scales

©2007 C. Harvey Publications All Rights Reserved.

Scale Studies (One String) for the Violin, Part One: One-Octave Scales ©2007 C. Harvey Publications All Rights Reserved.

B♭ major

A string

Scale Studies (One String) for the Violin, Part One: One-Octave Scales ©2007 C. Harvey Publications All Rights Reserved.

Scale Studies (One String) for the Violin, Part One: One-Octave Scales ©2007 C. Harvey Publications All Rights Reserved.

E♭ major

D string

Scale Studies (One String) for the Violin, Part One: One-Octave Scales

Scale Studies (One String) for the Violin, Part One: One-Octave Scales ©2007 C. Harvey Publications All Rights Reserved.

Scale Studies (One String) for the Violin, Part One: One-Octave Scales

F# major

E string

Scale Studies (One String) for the Violin, Part One: One-Octave Scales

Scale Studies (One String) for the Violin, Part One: One-Octave Scales

©2007 C. Harvey Publications All Rights Reserved.

B major

A string

Scale Studies (One String) for the Violin, Part One: One-Octave Scales
©2007 C. Harvey Publications All Rights Reserved.

E major

D string

Scale Studies (One String) for the Violin, Part One: One-Octave Scales

Scale Studies (One String) for the Violin, Part One: One-Octave Scales

©2007 C. Harvey Publications All Rights Reserved.

A major

G string

F# harmonic minor

E string

B harmonic minor

A string

Scale Studies (One String) for the Violin, Part One: One-Octave Scales

©2007 C. Harvey Publications All Rights Reserved.

E harmonic minor

D string

A harmonic minor

G string

Scale Studies (One String) for the Violin, Part One: One-Octave Scales ©2007 C. Harvey Publications All Rights Reserved.

F# melodic minor

E string

B melodic minor

A string

Scale Studies (One String) for the Violin, Part One: One-Octave Scales

©2007 C. Harvey Publications All Rights Reserved.

E melodic minor

D string

A melodic minor

G string

Scale Studies (One String) for the Violin, Part One: One-Octave Scales

©2007 C. Harvey Publications All Rights Reserved.

also available from www.charveypublications.com:
CHP185
Finger Exercises for the Violin, Book One

1

High Second Finger

Cassia Harvey

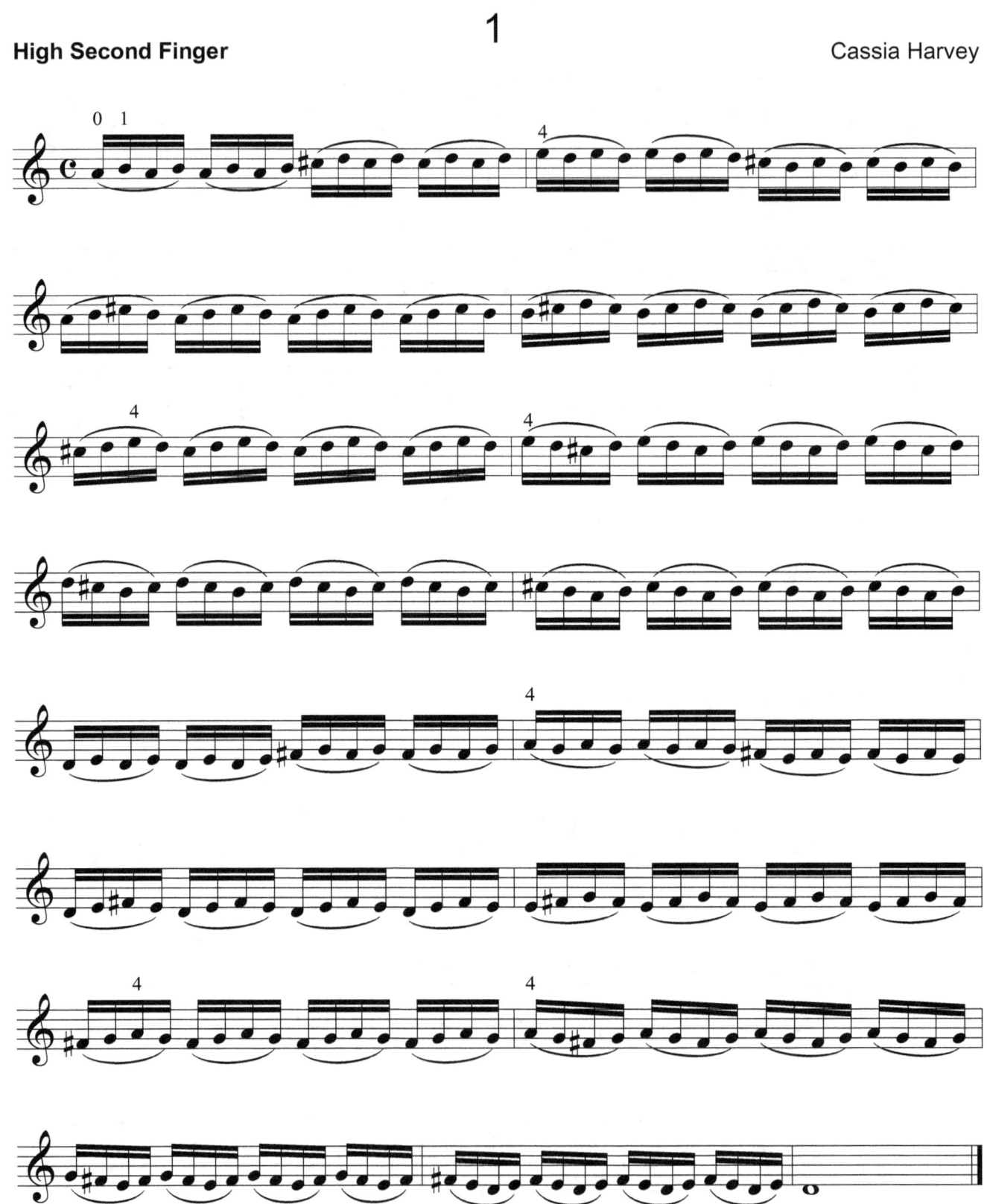

©2009 C. Harvey Publications All Rights Reserved.